THE WALLACE LINE

BY THE SAME AUTHOR

Borobudur (Transit Lounge, 2009)

Navigable Ink (Transit Lounge, 2020)

THE WALLACE LINE

A POEM

JENNIFER MACKENZIE

MELBOURNE, AUSTRALIA
www.transitlounge.com.au

First published 2025
Transit Lounge Publishing

Cover image: *Tracing the Wallace Line; wing leaf and land* by John Wolseley
Cover design: Peter Lo
Typeset in 11/14pt Bembo by Cannon Typesetting
Author image: Jian He, MSS Image

Printed in Australia by Pegasus Media and Logistics

A cataloguing-entry is available from the
National Library of Australia
ISBN: 978-1-923023-44-4

For Zeno and Holly

Contents

Section Three: Modernism

Section Four: The Wallace Line

Epilogue

Votive Offering

that time in Jogja
the hotel balcony on Sosrowijayan
rain thick as a curtain
the sugared tea sweet as –

tonight we'll go & dine
at a hotel for the rich
then I'll wrap you
in yards of spun cloth

I'll take you back east
to the one who called your name
as he built your true forest home

we'll stay there among the ruins

till our fingertips

can no longer bear it

SECTION ONE

Banda/Venice

BANDA I

And we had sailed and sailed to here be dragons
we came to shore late morning
and looking up into a thickly wooded panorama
we saw placed among it the white glow
of glorious *perkenier* housing
their pillars and gaudy casements looking out, as the poet said,
on a rich man's flowering lawns... his planted hills
& at one such dwelling a banquet in preparation
an aroma of spices packed into fresh-caught perch
gushing from the brazier
along a path to the slave quarters, bondsmen & bondswomen
brandishing bamboo nutmeg pickers
reaching high to the canopy of flourishing kenari trees
& the drying room, near as tall as those trees, towered above
great flames leapt to the brazier, men balancing on a high platform
raking the nuts on the drying trays &
men laden with sacks carried this black gold to the port

it was cool under the trees
almost cold
we shivered
a damp breeze
it is the presence of the anguished, said our guide.

II

he sat on the veranda
sipping a madeira
looking up
at the volcano

III

& we returned
was it seconds or centuries later?
the grand houses still stood there frozen in time
like unwanted guests perched along old pathways
some intact, their bougainvilleas flourishing
some nothing more than a wall of stone among the weeds
a government building lay empty
a ballroom with its marble floor bereft of waltzes & gin
its shutters creaking in the empty air
& the old drying room, collapsed at its centre
a tangled fish net of ruin
its outer poles still standing
a staircase leading to empty space, a drop of metres

& then we heard a singing sound
a singing sound
a vapour from the tall trees
first a lamentation
then a howling
an occluded cloud clinging to our clothes.

MALUKU PRISMATIC

the colour is luminous here
memory is of pastel
blue, pink, lemon robes in the marketplace
dwellings a slash of yellow & mauve
a constellation of red roofs
dimming only for star showers

on a clear night

CLOVE

NUTMEG

& the boats came
would they tip off the edge
of the earth
that edge sharp as glass

the volcano broods like a giant cat

Wallace's Birdswing butterflies ablaze
on a hot tropical day
storm clouds coming
on the day of the knife

kaleidoscope of fluttering tangerine wings
the deaths were silent

perpetrators

here in the shadow-rich square
the blood sacrifice lingers
a howling of *hantu*
flick of a presence
over the shoulders
a gossamer of spiders

FLYING

(for Nukila Amal)

Nukila took a dragon to fly over ancestral lands,
or should I say, her *narrator* took a dragon
what should I take, the flying bed of childhood,
the Flying Cot?
or plunge deep into the *cauchemar* of shopping malls,
their geometry confusing,
their escalators propped onto the precipice?

or flood right now
standing at the prow into pristine morning light
the blue of calm,
its warm moist air lightly flapping the sail?

the scent of cloves fragrant in the breeze
their near black, dusky flower

on the shoreline scratching my fingernails into mud & sand
flecks of clove dust concocting an alphabet
from the fragment of a dream

she puts the time-shift up a gear
landing lightly
enters her old home surprising her parents,
rummaging among the curled up sepia photographs
gathering fruit from the garden plot

it was the black gold that brought them
we fled to the mountain foothills
smoking Gamalama

swinging on the rusty gate

Your fingers smoking with letters
(for Nukila Amal)

clove infusion to the skin (marrow)
volcano above the head
clove grove to the body
salt sea skin fish to the toes
sea wrack to the boat sailing
a billowing of sulphur
clove mingling with its
huffery puffery
its majesty in dreams
its obliteration

you, and your dragon-headed prows
your porcelain & ceramics
your silks, your opium…
                    your discretion

you, and your camel trains
your ruby-encrusted swords, your perfumes,
your drums…
                    your honour

& you, your salt-soaked sails
your muskets, your cannons,
your gunpowder
                    your massacres.

SOUK

1. Colours

I came to a city unknown to me
a city of laneways & water
I wandered about, a ghost
following elusive pathways
enclosed within dark walls,
a splash of red enticed me,
an early glimmer
as a host of paintings
decorating church walls
took leave of their bondings,
merging bright oils
in the watery gloom of evening -
reds, blues, pinks – detached
from all representation
dissolved in mist,
rendering sky as palimpsest;
sunset blazed above me
then faded behind cloud,
I continued to wander
my destination unclear,
unreachable.

2. Souk

Frankenthaler flooded the colour…

the souk held the colours of Petra
paprika, saffron, cumin
fragrant among the rich glow
of intricately woven carpet

& at the entrance
the melody of an oud
floating in a cloud of melancholy
          rivers of longing,   into the blue

the souk held sacks of black pepper
coming from Malabar and beyond
over treacherous oceans
flavoured with the scent of sea salt and violets

& ginger loaded onto camels
coming out of Chang'an, city of dervishes,
through Turpan, city of musicians, grapes
and abundant wine, over deserts unending…

& as if by exchange of hand
a transformation
into floating domes, minarets,
mirrors and trompe-l'œil

in one such palace
with its bronze figure in the portico
its halo above
a flurry of Arcadian landscapes
Oh the Pastoral!

3. Venice

a palazzo can evoke
those heady days of trade & sea water
buzz of pastoral & tempest
dripping from the walls of
a masterpiece of churches
Marco Ricci's sfumato ignites
casts a palpable excitement
to the surface of the waterways
a lapping at crystal high tide

seasons dazzle
the orphan's bow a buoyant scoring
Vivaldi skips, knows
he's on to something.

4. Vivaldi The Four Seasons Spring Opus 8 No 1

& in the latter days,
Venice now a backwater
European flags planted all over distant shores,
when nostalgia became culture
nutmeg still bloomed as Spring
nymphs & shepherds leapt to dance
the sky full of birdsong, the
scent of new grasses
a sprightly violin taking up dance & lightning
a swarm of bees thick as black pepper
the oud entering the orchestra
a brio of ornamentation

as distant melody
a gamelan,
in the moonlight a Balinese dancer, bondswoman
& nutmeg picker, promised that Spring,
with all its variations,
would survive.

*

ARTIST'S MATERIALS

oltremare de Venezia

verdigris   vermillion
lead tin yellow   bone black
mosaic gold

                    lapis lazuli
          from central Asia
          the roaring of horses

think Fra Angelico, think Piero della Francesca,
think Leonardo,

think Titian

the artist's studio
window letting in the light
easel, brushes, palette, sheaves of sketches

fishing up these jewels
feels like last gasp retrieval

                              obsidian
     a mirror refracting   blue

SECTION TWO

The Silk Road

THE OUD IN TURPAN

the oud in Turpan
moonlight at the Moorish hotel
sound pure as water

NEW ENERGY

New Energy

crunched lavender stone of day
in times past jade invading horsemen
flew over these steppes
diving hawks, banners of war
howling from the mountain
on the grey day
pastures fertile as
recently as my boyhood
said the bus driver
crunch of pebbles under foot
not a camel or goat in view little breeze
lazily humming
wind turbines to the horizon
highway to
a future bright...

Khotan

To Khotan
for jade
desert power pouring its
thirst into the immortal

The wishing trees'
tangled roots holding
plant and soil together
are long gone
the worker leaves for lunch
an hour later his
sand-coated desk
blows towards him

Uighur Music

in Urumqi near the
market arcades, stalls of
melon crescents, smoking skewers
flying carpets
the oud fills
an ornate multi-level cranberry
scented cafe
with the longing of the caravan
crowds applauding the
silver singer's coded defiance
smoke rising from the copper kitchen
clocks set to local time
when bread is political

Dictionary

at the mosque two divergent schools
the first Uighur dictionary c1077
learn from the written word
or no learning
but from the experience of
the imminent of
what is apprehended
in sight and feeling between
chasm of house and hewn granite
whichever way
a hunger grows
from what is unsighted
on the highways of sand

Alien Coal/Corn

air pollution
the black humour plan
dig for coal in the West
but (ruefully) said
the Greenpeace activist
coal swallowing water
like a demon who knows
only thirst
Shrinking water table
somewhere on the road
between Korla and Aksu
a metre wide oasis
bubbling brook
a blaze of sunflowers
lush, sprightly corn
a soft buffeting breeze
a boy there
and the iron rocks of the wasteland
telling you:
it is us and only us

Dunhuang

at the Mogao grottoes
gold tribute from the Uighurs and
the Khotanese
is coloured on the rocky walls
here it was that General Yichao 848AD
forced back the Tibetans
Tang silk
fluttering in a victory breeze
and here it was Wang Wei said drink up,
from here on, there will be no good friends
and Li Bai: we go grey
holding our beacons of war
over the snowy-capped Pamirs
as for the donkeys,
they are weary of carting red chillies

Deserts Universal
(for Gigi Scaria)

at Dunhuang
the sands parted
for the explorer
unveiling the celestial
Avolokitesvara
blue and gold-leafed
camels harrumph
and lie down
arrogance flies off
for a short break

grey silent desert
you open up, and
reveal a city
alive on the draftsman's table

grey water wave-marked
moves over
salt crystal's glittering light
at dusk
an amber sedimentary glow
salt heaps wait
for trucks to scoop
motoring on the horizon

WHEN DU FU VISITED HE WAS UNFAZED

when Du Fu visited he was unfazed
by the amenities of a twenty-first century apartment
approved of the gas jets &
sat down for a dinner of fish & colourful vegetables
none of which he recognised
though he did compliment me on the wine
tenderly delivered from the limestone coast

until
the television screen flashed on for News
as flood waters raged in western Queensland
muddied overflow leaving roads impassable
he said, I have seen exactly that

but then cut to Syria
saw screaming children
mercy rescuers crying 'Allahu Akbar!'
as bombs, yellow chemicals rained down
on benighted Eastern Ghouta
then on to cratered Kabul
half-alive bodies in bloodied bandages

he said, I have seen just this
mud-sluiced valleys full of abandoned corpses
the heads of horses & oxen spiked with arrows
shards of bone rising to the light
in abject war-fashioned mementos

I was forced to tell him
that An Lushan was not the end of it
that the frontier was still fraught & vengeful
that the Bamiyan statues he had so longed to visit
were now but dust
leaving only an Image

as there was a spectacularly orange sunset
we thought we would sit on the balcony for a smoke
then quickly realised we needed something stronger

our eyes large light-filled buttons
whose lids held
the greater tears?

SECTION THREE

Modernism

MODERNISM

Gods float in the azure air
Pound much taken with Vivaldi & there's
Canto LXXV a Jannequin delight:
Gerhart
art thou come forth out of Phlegethon?
Gerhart, placed in Dresden,
btw he was no fascist.
Pound, Rudge and Munch their festival trajectory:
Vivaldi resplendent –
Siena/Venezia
forgotten now of course
their politics being as they were.
that EP washed up there

at the entrepot

and the palace hangs there in the dawn

SAILING

I love Conrad because he navigates the abyss, and doesn't sink into it.

Italo Calvino

he that was formed out of the icy gulag of exile
the remedy was to sail
languages, steeped in deep jungle, formed the heart

composing English to the strength of what he fashioned
BUT
the tales of others were best
the leisurely chat at dockside, beers & tobacco
the yarn cloaking the cruel, red-faced bluster of
European thieves

it was English that laced the forests & waterways
the sailors' homes, the beer & rum spiked with cigar ash
English flooded the yarn – a polyphony of sorts –
the immensity of sea & sky
actors mining duplicity or not, the flawed watchful in
his presence
set for a fall

Marlow, Tiresias
I, Tiresias
I, Ganesha, I, Marlow.

set for a fall
& at the source of the river
dark foliage, a fiery sun

monkeys chattering on water's edge
all saying, continue *in*
to be flung – lover of trees –
to be torpedoed at mad pace
the body rising embracing sapling & bark
skin shedding all memory
a disgrace pocketed
yes, the Achilles heel –
in the slime, a welcome in weed & bog

oh Jim, dominating the page the furtive estuary
I, the author...

walking down Collins Street
I'd never felt so alone
JC 1888

try
early morning a Sunday
Elizabeth Street, 1969
one furtive café
OPEN

a light blinks
above its bain-marie

VICTORY: AN ISLAND TALE

he took it upon himself
the rescue -
Heyst
wedged into silence
like a Pharaoh in a tomb
took it upon himself
the girl and her violin
the instrument passport and bondage
both
took her to his island
to what he thought
was their true forest home
how he marvelled -
her delicacy
her restless eyes, her fear

away from the women's orchestra
her pink faced pursuers -
it was a dream
his emotion he could not fathom…
floundering
what to say to her
he, condemned to what
to meaning, living,… love?

significant dread
came upon the boats one dawn
the hunters
evil flooding out of them
like ink upon the world

ALMAYER

Almayer's small hut
Verdi's *Il Trovatore* floating over
treetops & waterways
he'd longed for Europe & the grand entrée
a good house on the canal paintings on the walls
his want cost him
waiting for Tattslotto to hit
in the wilds of Kalimantan
diamonds did not drop

forest & river a unity of susurration
frangipani blossoming in radiant damp
a silver light from the moon
catching glitter & sparkle
the Balinese youth's jewelled anklet
Almayer's daughter & her lover
their canoe, the moon drifting,
now a smudge on the horizon

alone,
his daughter gone,
with a couple of bats
circling above his head
the opium pipe awaits
too poor an outcome
hubris wrapping him in its sorry cloud
too bad, if he hadn't been such a fool,
in another life
he could have sailed on

become dotty Dad
a corner in a Balinese compound
storm
an uprooted tree
its supplicating branches
spin out to sea.

BLUR

My first sight of Almayer:
a blurred figure barely discernible
among low mist & jungle
rounding a bend in the river
emerging as we did out of thick fog
moisture dripping from every rope on board
bamboo & palm in slow rain
an umbrella over muddy pathways
we struggled to find a foothold.

If I hadn't met Almayer
not a word of mine would
have been in print
your name, floating over equatorial
bars & sailors' homes
your name, fate's calamity

I took you into what was to become
my writing self
embodying your want of sense
born on murmuring seas
I left the vain shadow of your existence
left it on the river along with mine

somewhere in the Indian Ocean reading Salammbo

not a word...
it began with what became Chapter 10
while iced up on a quay in Rouen

& while in Geneva at the hydropathic centre
Chapter 8
the whole thing yellowing over
many ocean voyages
my fate & yours
almost lost leaving my bag
at a station back in Ukraine
not a word without you
thc two of us, sad fools,
incorrigible, hopeless Don Quixote

ADELAIDE

(for Judy Morris and Ian Gibbins)

JC 1892
convalescing in the Adelaide Hills
among the magpies & koalas
& to graziers' wives for lunch

then there were the fires

decades later
damp & smoke settling over the eucalyptus
my friend J nurses
a lost & singed koala
seasons pass, but the koala returns
nestling in J's lap

convalescing in the Adelaide Hills
JC a palpable sense of light & dark
J, hours spent, a pencilled truth to canvas
Truth, JC wrote, *the pencilled robe of imagined phrases.*

SYDNEY

here, everything is known of everybody
a cluster of vagabondage

Sydney, town of my youthful affection:
Because Of The Dollars
A spectre of the handless Frenchman
a tobacco shop in George Street, 1878

MELBOURNE

in Melbourne on the *Otago*
a cargo of teak
in Melbourne

never   so   alone.

KALIMANTAN

(for Emmanuela Shinta)

the lure of diamonds brought them initially
mangroves slink into the peatlands
chainsaw & caterpillar tractor
leaching tannins

a burning smell like no other

hutan
bukan hanya milik kita
hutan

canals dug deep
megaphone forest clearance
ironwood logs illegally cut

a tangle of weed & nothingness

palm oil plantations to the horizon
to the azure oceans of

PLASTIC

*

burning burning burning
smoke haze twenty years of
but this is a different smell
I pick the wild fruit and it is bitter
Oh sweet taste of my youth

you can hear the breathing
the soft voice of elders
in the heart of this place
the forests are burning
pollution index 2000+

peatlands burning
particles of death
to the lungs

here at the heart
we are helpless
without succour

through winding road to the heart we go
a convoy of motorcyclists deep into the centre

winding
road
motorcycle
diaries
to
the
peatlands

the journey was long

into hovering death
haze thick

oh our dripping jackets
oh our clinging skirts

what we can offer
masks, medicines, a fan of toothbrushes

rubber trees, blissful sandalwood ash collateral
setting up a kitchen for the firefighters

a burning smell like no other

our motorcycle diaries
honeycombed in trauma
written in charcoal *mourned in blood*

*

Conrad's brooding bar on the river

melancholy

out of Bangkok

and into

____

WHAT PLACE

*

floating in the *klotok*
down the river
walls of pandanus, lianas
closing in
hair damp from broadleaf spray
eyesight entering a darkness
clotted by drip & cloud

hutan
bukan hanya milik kita
hutan

Oh delight
Hallelujah Chorus:
gibbons, clouded leopards, sun bears, giant crimson-winged
butterflies, hornbills, tarsiers, frisky freshwater dolphins, the odd croc

are they here
a company rising above the clouds
or is it merely the hand passing through a membrane

to yesterday's visionary splendour

the forest
not only us
the forest

Kalimantan, from the Sanskrit
Kalamanthana,
Burning weather island

RIMBAUD

(in memory of Jamie James)

Sunda Kelapa, Batavia
In the port city of B
wandering at night
subterranean hotel & docklands
red velvet interior
the phantom proprietor
rang for the heavenly moon & service

in the chill bar
chairs facing
the ocean's monsoonal heat
wild vagabond
a glass of bad wine
string of grapes around his fingers
saying:
I live in this cavern
and ask
that you do not abandon
my body
that you can see in its
musculature
the grey and bronze
patterns of the bacchante.

Semarang
After a proud tour of the
spice godowns
KNIL march across Java
rice fields & jungle
sway to the colonial Boot

Salatiga barracks
bugle & torment
equatorial downpour
uniform a puddle on the floor
I make an exit in mufti

now hiding in this thatched grotto
en route to Semarang & you
made up a story for the brother-in-law:
hid in the jungle for months
w/ kindly tigers, chattering apes.

ARTAUD AND THE ECSTATIC TRANSFER

Exposition colonial internationale, Paris 1931

'Who am I?
Where do I come from?
I am Antonin Artaud
and I say this
as I know how to say this
immediately
you will see my present body
burst into fragments
and remake itself
in ten thousand notorious
aspects'

and how does time flow?
the gesture/s and the fan
flickering across continents
                                        the gamelan's
ecstatic pinning of the minimal and the decorative
to a percussive consciousness
pirouette through the horizontal mirror of fingers
fly into theatre's mango grove and
marketplace   where
the golden heart outlives winter

transparent pick of the gamelan

*

the priest predicted rain
for this afternoon
and it is gently falling

over the rice-fields
over bright lamplight
rain a soft gauze
onto the black night
crickets chirp, geckos
dart over walls, seeking
secret hiding places
among columns of insects
marching over plants
refreshed and sensible to light

*

from the black and ruined forest
the dancer springs
frontally illuminated
swaddled chrysalis
fingers flickering butterfly wings
defiant of the
dark unspoken gloom of
trees, mountains withholding
unnavigable springs
frantic hollow drumbeats score
a gestured metaphysic
mirrored interplay of
moonrise eyes, pouting lips
head travelling shoulder to shoulder
as if on rollers
rain singing over instruments
sharded flights of sound

inflected, airborne from the back of the throat
syncopated feet, hot and dexterous
stamping crackling leaves and twigs
from a percussive earth
conjuring dry seething plants
gulping rain,
beckon the ecstatic drummer

*

ballroom where the
lover-dance
undid me
waltzing over snow
in flaming sunset

*

the gamelan of death
is coming along the river bank
I hide in a hollow   from
wild unleashed
I place the mask over the collapsing
portraiture
mask and its double
I am the fearful aspect of
the Tiger, I am – and do not question it –
this spectacle
I   am   an   other

BALI 2005

Amitav Ghosh, Michael Ondaatje
a conversation
looking over a languorous Lombok Strait
mist rising from the sea
palms swaying as if dancing the legong

to the Wallace Line

SECTION FOUR

The Wallace Line

THE WALLACE LINE

obtaining a passage on a Bugis prahu
I took the long journey to the island of Aru
excited as a schoolboy
I laid claim to my cabin on board
a delight of thatch & bamboo
I felt as sheltered as if in
a hut in the jungle
at night stars & ocean glowed
in a diamond light
& when dawn arrived
it was as if I was breathing in
the very beginning of the world

pondering the absence of thrush
& oriole, my head full of birdsong
a panorama of the honeyeater, the white cockatoo,
the Bird of Paradise that awaits

the next evening
stepping ashore at Banda
I take the path through town to
the Governor's residence
a procession of glass-covered street lamps
guiding my way
grasped a moment at a stall
to quench my thirst
fished out the notebook
a constellation of images, an Idea
forming, stuttering its way through the dark

LOMBOCK

'At length, about four o'clock, the Pumbuckle made his appearance, and we informed him of our desire to stay with him for a few days, to shoot birds and see the country.'
Alfred Russell Wallace, *The Malay Archipelago,* p. 183

into the interior, & then low hills,
terraced rice fields
& to what we saw was a paradise of a garden
tobacco, cucumbers, yams & beans,
with streams running over moss-covered stones

waiting for the Pumbuckle
kingfishers of a violet & orange hue
graced trees at the edge of a small
yet shady forest
kingfishers, yes, so like the Australian bird,
the glorious Laughing Jackass

thought of this & other quandaries,
notebook flourishing,
the day dragged on without resolution
we spent the night in a cold pavilion
barely fed, too odd to be believed.

JAVA: JOURNEY TO THE INTERIOR

'Mr Bell drove me over to the village of Modjo-ogong, where
he was building a house and premises for the tobacco trade',
TheMalay Archipelago, p117

travelling east & was confounded by what I saw   buried in lofty
forests temples, tombs, statues   radiating a perfection from which
the sun & moon equally appeared to glow   in a soft & radiant light

on a trip searching for birds   we passed a torrent of bubbling &
steaming water   a hill above of overhanging ferns & lycopodia
just visible through the drizzling rain

climbing down from Kadang Barak   our guide said the Tiger,
the Rhinoceros & the Wild Bull roam here at will   indeed as we
passed more ruins I spied   a Tiger stretched upon a plinth of stone
sunning itself & with no interest in us

back in my rooms thanks to the hospitality of the local regent
I admired my catch   a peacock & a rare green jungle fowl
graced by a violet comb   a red blue & yellow wattle hanging
beneath the throat

gamelan played all night   gongs & drums a hypnotic syncopation
the moon glowing above the musicians   clutched my gift of a
Durga statue   never underestimate the generosity of others

back on the road something happened as we passed Mount Arjuna
my head began to throb   blood coursing through my veins like
lava released into a river   looking out over cultivated fields   my
eyesight felt occluded   as if seeing only half the picture

WALLACE: MALUKU

sneered at as a mere flycatcher
I have no mind
what danced before my sight
what I found: The Wallace Line
is all delight

*

6AM	**TEA**
7AM	**TEA EGGS SARDINES**
10AM	**MADEIRA GIN & BITTERS**
11AM	**LARGE BREAKFAST**
3PM	**TEA COFFEE**
5PM	**DINNER**
6.30PM	**BEER CLARET**
8PM	**TEA COFFEE**
ALL DAY	**BEER SODA WATER WHATEVER**

Dutch ships float comfortably

*

Banda

the sky diamond clear
transparent coral
fish, all colours of the rainbow
seven fathoms deep

for how long?

the bare cone of the volcano
black vertical lines of water gullies
a dense sulphur cloud above
brooding in the damp
a tangle of climbing rattans
festooned over fern & palm

incomparable Nutmeg!
the Fruit Pigeon's booming call
Sheltered by the Kanary tree
bathed in tropical rain

a yellow flower
a nut the colour of peach
and a band of crimson mace

Oh such beauty!
Oh such delight!

Amboya

sleeping rooms in my bamboo hut
all night slumbering above me
a Python

only the entomologist
can share my delight
hunting Butterflies in hot sunshine

Ternate

Ternate, you earthquake wracked island
mountains flourishing dense
with durian, mango, mangosteen
the Sultan's palace half a ruin

gold, emeralds, spices
earthquake: the land
moving like a sea

the white Cockatoos screech
around my hut
drying feathered specimens

my pins & labels
my hand lenses
how I admire Beetles, Parrots
& Hornbills

Aru

on a tree
twenty or more
Birds of Paradise
branches & leaves vibrate
almost a humming

Oh cinnabar King Bird of Paradise
smaller than a Thrush

as clear and lacquered as a gem
what more do I need to see?

*

on the ship home
food for my Birds was scarce
I hunt all night
for a black scattering of
Cockroaches

*

sneered at as a mere flycatcher
my sleep invaded like an
earthquake from Ternate
regretting the harm I did
too late!
cadavers of my specimens
shriek & flutter
pecking as if I, a
monster corpse.

TREPANG

(in memory of Lily Yulianti Farid)

and we came to the bustling streets of M----
we spied among the crowd tall, curly-haired men, decorated
with a design unknown to us
& drenched in a vermillion sunset so wondrous it seemed a
blessing from heaven
we returned to the port dense with the majestic phinisi
& we were told they were trepang traders
dwellers on a coastline far away
an immense country beyond imagination &
with animals as if from an almanac
what kind?

hopping deer
laughing birds.

Epilogue

LEE MINGWEI: THE MOVING GARDEN

(for Tess Rice)

the flowers pour in from the market gardens
rest in a gentle spiral in the trough
the artist requests
that a viewer pluck a flower
take some circuitous route
to their next port of call &
gift the bloom to a stranger

such

momentary intensity of the chance encounter, or

could the flower go to another artist
the photographer
revealing her creations to the world
this very afternoon?

somewhere else
the painter exhibits
in a building up for demolition
portraits segue into the ruins
the dim light from high windows
beaming into the shadows
catching red in the spotlights

could it too carry the gift of the floral?

NOTES

Banda sequence: in 1621 mercenaries under Jan Pieterszoon Coen committed genocide of the people of Banda, ensuring a Dutch monopoly on the spice trade. A pattern of massacre and ecocide, including the wholesale destruction of clove plantations, was characteristic of Dutch domination. Prior to that the trade in spices had proceeded for centuries with China, India, the Middle East, and on to Venice.

Perkenier is the owner of the nutmeg estates (there's one left apparently), quotation *the rich man's flowering lawns, his planted hills*, From Ancestral Houses, in *Collected Poems of W.B. Yeats*, (Macmillan 1967).

The most significant reference for this collection is the writings of Amitav Ghosh, in particular *The Nutmeg's Curse*, John Murray 2021. Another pertinent source is the novel by Hanna Rambe, *Mirah of Banda*, trans Toni Pollard, Lontar 2010

Flying and Your Fingers Smoking with Letters: Nukila Amal is an Indonesian writer. In her prize winning novel *Cala Ibis* (translated into English as *The Original Dream* trans Linda Owens, Amazon Crossing 2007) the narrator travels by dragon to eastern Indonesia. The text in italics in the poems, including the title of *Your fingers smoking with letters* are quotations from the novel.

Souk: this sequence is inspired by oud player Joseph Tawadros's collaboration with the Australian Chamber Orchestra, in a performance of Vivaldi's Four Seasons.

On the theme of musicological connection, I recommend Mathias Enard's wonderful novel, *Compass*, trans. Charlotte Mandell (Fitzcarraldo 2017).

Marco Ricci, Italian painter (1676-1730). His paintings are said to have inspired Vivaldi.

Artist's Materials: list of painters and their materials from Peter Frankopan, *The Silk Roads*, Bloomsbury 2016, p.179

Uighur Music: in Xinjiang province both Beijing and local time operate.

Deserts Universal: Gigi Scaria is an Indian artist. This poem references *Dust*, his exhibition at the Ian Potter Museum 2013.

The explorer referred to is Aurel Stein, the first European to 'discover' the Dunhuang caves.

When Du Fu Visited He was Unfazed: inspired by biographical details of Du Fu, in Boey Kim Cheng's novel, *Gull Between Heaven and Earth*, Epigram Books, 2017

Modernism: references to Ezra Pound, *The Cantos*, Canto III, XXV, and LXXV, Faber, London, 1975

Conrad poems: references from Italo Calvino, *Why Read the Classics*, Penguin 2009, Conrad's *A Personal Record*, Duke Classics n.d., first published 1912, *Lord Jim*, Penguin 2012, first published 1900, *Almayer's Folly*, Penguin 2002, first published 1895, *Victory: An Island Tale*, Penguin 2015, first published 1915, Ian Burnet, *Joseph Conrad's Eastern Voyages*, Alfred Street

Press, 2021, Martin Edmond, *Marlowe's Dream: Joseph Conrad in Antipodean Ports*, Index Press 2024, Edward Said, *Joseph Conrad and the Fiction of Autobiography*, Columbia University Press 2008. In the poem *Victory: an Island Tale.* The lines he, condemned to what/*to meaning, living, love* from the forward by Andrew N Rubin to Said: "Said's emphasis on the phenomenological preoccupation (being condemned to meaning) and the existential predicament (being condemned to living) provides the coordinates of an antimony…that gets transposed in the works themselves" pp. 14–15, *"significant dread"*, Said, op.cit. p. 8

Judy Morris, neuroscientist and artist, and Ian Gibbins, neuroscientist, poet and video artist live in the Adelaide Hills.

Kalimantan. Emmanuela Shinta is a writer, artist, film maker and environmental activists. Material from her organisation, the Ranu Welum Foundation, is referenced in the first section of the poem www.ranuwelum.org

Rimbaud: details of Arthur Rimbaud's march across Java and desertion from the army: Jamie James, *Rimbaud in Java, The Lost Voyage*, Didier Millet 2011

Jamie James, American writer (1951–2020)

Artaud and the Ecstatic Transfer: response to Antonin Artaud's essay *On the Balinese Theatre* 1931, in *The Theatre and its Double*, trans M.K. Richards, Grove 1958, first published 19380 and to a dance piece, *Artaud*, choreographed by Ni Made Pujawati and Ash Mukherjee Artaud.mov – YouTube https://www.youtube.com/watch?v=XOGu8z5uGKQ

Bali 2005. From an interview with Amitav Ghosh, he says "A memory that lingers particularly is a conversation with Michael Ondaatje...overlooking the Lombok Strait, through which runs the Wallace Line." Ubud Writers & Readers Festival Newsletter, posted 7 October 2024.

The Wallace Line section: based on Alfred Russell Wallace's *The Malay Archipelago*, Penguin 2014, originally published 1869, in particular Volume Two. See also Ian Burnet's marvellous *Where Australia Collides with Asia*, Rosenberg 2017, John Wolseley, *Tracing the Wallace Line, exhibition catalogue* Bendigo Art Gallery, 2001. Alfred Russell Wallace (1823–1913), naturalist and explorer. The Wallace Line is a faunal boundary between Bali and Lombok.

Lombock: Pumbuckle: a district head

Trepang: Lily Yulianti Farid (1971-2023) was a writer, co-founder of the Makassar International Writers Festival, and an academic.. The poem is based on research from Monash University"s Global Encounters Unit. Trepang were traded between northern Australia and Indonesia for hundreds of years before the trade was banned by the Australian Government in 1907.

A report on ABC News featured this research, in particular the search for descendants of Aboriginal people who settled in Indonesia at least 150 years ago, and the discovery of photographs in an Italian library of what has been identified as being of Yolgnu men in Makassar: https://www.abc.net.au/news/2023-02-11/mystery-community-of-aboriginal-and-indonesian-families/101901188

Lily, who features in the report, was working on this project at the time of her death.

trepang is sea cucumber, phinisi is a Makassan boat

Lee Mingwei is a Taiwanese/American artist. His installation, The Moving Garden, was exhibited at the National Gallery of Victoria, 2016/17

Tess Rice is a Melbourne based photographer.

The painter referred to in the poem is Rone, a Melbourne based artist.

ACKNOWLEDGEMENTS

The Wallace Line: A Poem had its beginnings over ten years ago when I came across a painting by John Wolseley, titled *The Wallace Line,* in the storeroom of the Australian Galleries in Melbourne, and it fostered an interest over the years that has found form in this book. I am very grateful indeed, and thank John for so generously providing the cover image.

I am grateful for the generosity and support of so many friends in both Australia and Asia. A particular thank you to lifelong friends, Kris Hemensley, Kerry Murphy and Russell Grigg – my books would not have happened without you. Thanks to the members of the Indo Lit Club, coordinated by Toni Pollard, for our regular monthly sessions discussing Indonesian literature, and a special thanks to Toni for introducing me to the wonderful fiction of Nukila Amal. Thank you also to the support from the directors of writers' festivals, in particular Janet de Neefe and her team in Ubud, to Sabin Iqbal and his team in Trivandrum, and to Sally Breen and Asia Pacific Writers & Translators (APWT). I owe a great deal to the writings of Amitav Ghosh, in particular his *Nutmeg's Curse.* Ever since researching the world of eighth and ninth century Asia, I have been fascinated by the connection between culture and trade, and Ghosh's fine book has been an inspiration. And last and not least to Barry Scott and Tess Rice of Transit Lounge: huge gratitude for your ongoing support of my work.

Some of these poems have appeared in the following publications, sometimes in different form: *ACU Poetry Prize Chapbook: Empathy, Australian Poetry Anthology, 2021, Australian Poetry Journal 13.1, 2023, Eunoia Review (Singapore), Literary Shanghai, Plumwood Mountain Journal: Poets speaking up to Adani.*

The poems *Maluku Prismatic* and *Kalimantan* were originally published in *Navigable Ink* (Transit Lounge 2020).

Many of these poems were written on the unceded lands of the Wurundjeri-Woiwurrung people, and I pay my respects to elders past and present. I also pay respects to the Yolgnu people, referenced in the poem *Trepang,* to the Peramangk and Kaurna peoples (*Adelaide)* and Gadigal people (*Sydney*).

Jennifer Mackenzie lives in Naarm/Melbourne. *The Wallace Line: A Poem* is the third volume, following *Borobudur* and *Navigable Ink,* in a series exploring what has become the home of her Imagination, Indonesia. She has appeared at a number of conferences and festivals across Asia, most recently at the Ubud Writers Festival, and the Mathrubhumi International Festival of Letters in Trivandrum.